A KEEK INSIDE

Drawings by

George Martin

Published in 2007 by
Intro2 Publishing
55B Upper Brockley Road
London SE4 1SY

ISBN: 978-1-904865-06-3

Printed in the UK by Scotprint

Distribution by Intro2 Books.
http://www.intro2books.com

INTRODUCTION

In the early seventies, I had the privilege of working with George 'Spud' Martin in Smith & Hutton's Boatbuilders, Victoria Dock, Dundee. Spud was the perfect companion in what was often an imperfect environment; cold and damp. He called me 'The Moth' because I always found any source of heat like a magnet, and after a while I became 'The Singing Moth'. Spud's talent was obvious to us and all his workmates were very proud of him, which was a great pleasure to witness.

I remember a nice man called Boab Martin got a gaffer's job and he cut a familiar figure with his hands in the pockets of his duffel coat. Spud drew him on a plate with his hood up and the legend below…

THE BLACK ABBOT COMETH

I also enjoyed his company in the worker's occupation of Shed S during the boring part of Smith & Hutton's metamorphosis into a beautiful Kestrel Marine Ltd.

I am very pleased to see the completion of this third volume of Spud's unique observations and already look forward to his next one.

Michael Marra

Michael Marra is a Songwriter, Artist, Actor and Writer who has contributed to many Publications as well as Theatre and Television Productions.

Alec Andrex

Alec used to be a plater's helper in the boatyaird at the same time as I worked there, but then left when he got an opening with the Dundee Cleansing Dept as a 'Scaffy'. His beat was the Seagate.

One Saturday morning, while sleeping up some pend behind one of the big stores in the Seagate, he came across some tins of Corned Beef lying in a skip which had been thrown out a couple of days before. Alec said to himself, 'This'll do me!' without noticing that the tins were damaged and perforated. So he took them home and made a big pot of stovies for supper.

Alec lived above Anton's Bar on the Ferry Road. Saturday night was a big night in Anton's Bar and Alec was an important man in there. He was the M.C. in the Sing-Song Room. Saturday night was going well; good singers, bad singers, rotten singers, they were all there. The Bars closed at 9.30pm then, so some people used to get kerry-oots to go to house parties to carry on partying. That night, Alec announced, 'Everybody up to meh hoos fir a perty!' so everybody went upstairs to Alec's hoos. The party was going great-guns, when Alec mentioned that he had a rare treat for everybody. He had a big pot of stovies heating in the oven. 'So, grab a fork and knife and get stuck in.' Somebody seemingly shouted, 'Three cheers for Alec!' but then an hour later, they were shouting for his blood. Everybody at the party had a dose of the skitters. You couldn't get in a toilet in that tenement for love nor money. They were even shitting in the 'Backies'. For a couple of days after, folk were keeping their toilet-rolls in the fridge.

I see Alec nearly every morning now. He waits for his bus at the bottom of Craigie Avenue. He must be about 90 years old now. He sometimes wears a white neck-support which, when I remember back to his escapade with the Corned Beef, reminds me of a big toilet-roll.

Allan the Staple Boy

Allan is an old boatyaird man. He was an ex-riveter who also worked at the whaling in his younger days. When he retired a long time ago, he acquired a part-time job with an undertaker. He is still there to this day. His job entailed lining the coffins with some kind of material which he would staple to the inside of the box.

Although he was a part-time Undertaker's helper, Allan still liked to wear his old boatyaird boots to work. One day his boss caught him working inside a coffin with his boots on and he said to Allan in a solemn tone, 'Would you please refrain from wearing those dirty boatyaird boots, as someone's got to lie in that!'

Andy Broon

Andy Broon is another one of the old Dundee characters. He was famous for going all over Dundee collecting empty bottles. He had this great big sack and he would fill the sack 'til it was jam-packed with bottles. He would then try and get on the bus with it, but most times I don't think they let him on.

His main objective was 'The Bottily'. I don't know where the place was, but it was doon-the-toon somewhere. Anyway, he would get money for the empties. His famous saying to women was, 'Any empty bottles ladies please?'. One woman told me she shouted to him, 'I have some bottles for you, Andy.' And he shouted back, 'The bottily's closed today missus, I'm only collecting woollens today.' He was a man of many talents. Weekends he would sing in your 'backies' for extra cash and by some accounts he was pretty good.

Black Eck

Black Eck was a plumber in the boatyaird. They say that when he started in the yaird as a fifteen-year-old, he had this big bonnet on. He had a good head of hair yet this bonnet was always on his head. Someone told me he gets a new one every ten years which he would then take outside and rub in the muck and stoor to give it a much more 'used' look. He is not a dirty person, it's just that he was always doing 'homers' (jobs on-the-side) and had his working clothes on nearly all the time.

Somebody said they saw a photograph of Black Eck at primary school in Kirkton, and there he was in the front row with his big bonnet on.

Boaby the Plater

Boaby was a plater in the boatyaird boilershop. He always wore a beret and carried his hammer in his belt, that's how I would describe him.

In the boatyaird, they used to play some dirty tricks, and one was on Boaby. I don't know who did it, as I was only told about it. Boaby liked his can of tea, and used to look forward to it at the breaks. Well what happened was, someone found a dead mouse and slipped it into Boaby's rule-pocket, and when Boaby had his tea, out would come the steel-rule to give it a good stir. The prankster said to Boaby, 'You have to give it a good stir for a good brew.' The mouse was in his rule-pocket for months and must've eventually turned to dust. I dinna think it done him any harm, as he lived to a ripe old age.

Butch and the Black Diamonds

A long time ago Dundee had a great event called, 'The Five-A-Sides Football Competition.' There was the serious side to it and the funny side. They say there were hundreds who attended it. Well, I was never there but I've been told a few stories about it. One of the stories was about the famous Black Diamonds whose Captain and spearhead was the famous George 'Butch' Butchart. They were all Coal-men and they were the main attraction at 'The Fives'. As footballers, they weren't very good but they just got stuck-in. Their opponents were always asked to let Butch score a goal, and when he'd scored, the place erupted. You could hear the roar half-way across Dundee. Back then, Butch would pull the football strip over his head, (and they say Ravanelli, the Italian player copied it off Butch.) and would then take-off doing his lap of honour round Northend Park with hundreds of kids chanting 'Butch Butch Butch!'

Carry me on

As a welder in the boatyaird you got the name of being a bit lazy, especially from the platers. They used to say the welders always wanted things done for them and would shout things such as, 'get me this' and 'get me that'. Anyway I did this wee drawing a long time ago just to stir it up. A welder was getting carried about on this stretcher, and one lad said to the other, 'Has there been an accident?', and the other lad said, 'No, they're just carrying the welder to his next job.'

Charlie's Wellies

Charlie Ross was a labourer in the building trade. The story about Charlie was that he always wore wellies at work rest or play, and maybe even wore them to bed. Anyway Charlie passed away and the funeral took place at the crematorium. He had a big turnout, and after the service as the mourners were walking down the pathway from the Cremy (Crematorium), the people looked up at the thick black smoke coming from the chimney when some wag shouted out, 'They must have forgotten to take Charlie's wellies off!'

Dandy McClean

This story was told to me by an old mill-mechanic who worked in Tamson and Shepherd's jute mill in Taylors Lane, just off the Perth Road.

There was this lad called Jock who worked in a department where he did the dust shaking. In the Dundonian lingo, his job was a 'stoor-shakker'. I don't know what that entailed, but I think it must have been an unenviable task. Anyway, there was a security lad who didn't like Jock, and he was always trying to catch him taking something off the premises without permission. The security man's nickname was Dandy McClean, named after some detective who I think was in the Weekly News. Well one day he sees Jock (who has just finished his shift) carrying this bag, and Dandy thinks he has a capture. He demanded a look in the bag. As Jock opened the bag, Dandy quickly stuck his head in to have a look then collapses on the floor, gagging. Well it turned out that earlier on in the day Jock had shet ees breeks, so he stuck them in the bag and was taking them home to wash. Dandy's complexion seemingly looked the colour o' bad sassages for weeks after the bag incident, or so I was telt.

Dead Loss

Dead Loss was a likeable lad who worked as a Dundee Docker. I used to see him often in the passing. He always seemed to have a smile on his face. This was one of the stories I heard about him...

One lunch break he was in the Dockers Club, which was in the Ferry Road. Well, after he had his liquid lunch (which used to be about a gallon of beer) he headed back to the docks. They say he was working on the unloading of some German ship. He was working away, then a wee rumble down in the bowels department and then (bang) he shet ees breeks. He then immediately jumped overboard to cleanse himself. It was quite shallow as the tide was out, and he stood waist-deep in the water just looking up at the ship, smiling. The German Captain looked down at Dead Loss and said, 'No wonder you people won ze bloody war'.

Doctor Who

Doctor Who was a First-Aid man in the boatyaird, but he used to go a bit too far. He must have thought he was a real doctor, he had his own stethoscope and all types of doctory implements. He would lance boils, syringe ears, you name it and he would have a go. Some people would go to the ambulance room (as we called it,) for a wee skive but that all stopped when Doctor Who came to the boatyaird. People were scared to go there as they were more frightened of him than the infamous Nazi doctor, Josef Mengele.

Doctor Who must've had an accident of some sort because he had this queer stiff-backed gait when he walked. I don't like to make fun of anybody but that's just the way it was.

Anyway, the story was that some carpenter had had an accident in the yard down one the slipways, so Doctor Who made his way to the scene of the accident. The ambulance arrived at the same time and spotted him immediately, with that strange walk he had. They grabbed him, and put him in the ambulance. Doctor Who was screaming, 'I'm not the casualty you idiots, it's another lad down the slipway!' The real accident victim was recovering where he fell during all this time, and his mate said to him, 'You had a close shave there! Doctor Who nearly got to you first!'

Dundee's Dance Halls

When I was young, my pals and I would go out on Friday nights. We would go down the town and have a few drinks in The Neuk. At that time the pubs shut at 9.30pm so we would then head for The Pally, (Palais de Dance was its proper name.) where we would queue up to get in. When you got in to the Pally you would put your coats in the cloakroom, then go down the stairs for the last dance, and if you didn't get a lass, you went straight hame. What a braw life! Nowadays, the young anes don't go out 'til about midnight!

The Tonk (Empress Ballroon) was in Dock Street and that was a bit rougher than the Pally. There were loads of pubs all round that area, so you could imagine the clientele that entered The Tonk - they couldn't hardly walk let alone dance. There was always a load of punch-ups in there.

One that fascinated me was The Proagie (The Progress Hall) and it was on the Hulltoon. Some old-timers told me about it, and they say it was a right den of iniquity. I remember an old woman told me years ago that she was in The Proagie, when some lad asked her up to dance, and when she looked down at his feet, she saw that he had a big pair of wellies on. Another old lad who played the sax and worked in the boatyaird with me said that when there was a big punch-up, even the band got steamed in.

Gatox Tam

I was working nightshift with the firm Kestrel a long time ago and during our tea break I had a real goodie for the rest of the boys - a box that contained a big Black Forest Gateaux which I was given for doing a wee job for a lad. I think his wife had a shop that specialized in making them. Well I opened the box and sliced it up for the lads. A while later, Tam the gaffer came in declaring 'Tea break's over, get back to your joabs,' then he spotted the gateaux. 'What's that your eating, a gatox?' I said, 'Would you like a slice Tam?' He said me, 'I wouldn't put that keech anywhar near meh mooth!' So we all left the cabin and went back to our jobs. Five minutes later I realised I had left my welding gloves in the cabin, so when I arrived back at the cabin and opened the door, there was Tam, I couldn't see his pus for gatox.

Geordie The Electric Skaffy

My Grandfather came from the Stobswell area. I only remember him from when I was about eight years old. He was a big tall skinny man and he always worked as a skaffy. He lived in Catherine Street, in the Stobbie. I was told by my Granny that he was known as *The Electric Skaffy*. His area was Dundonald Street and Court Street. They say if you lived in a low-doon door (ground floor) and left your door open, he would come in and sweep yir hoos oot.

Give Me Death

A lad worked in the boatyaird with me and his name was Davy. He lived in Lillybank. I think he was just sixteen and he was going with a lass the same age. Well, as Dundonians would say, he put her 'in the club,' she was 'up the duff' or, 'in the pud'n club' or, 'she had a bun in the oven.' She was pregnant and she had a few big brothers and they waylaid Davy coming from the boatyaird as he turned into Lillybank Road. They gave him an ultimatum - Marry her or it's Death. He said, 'Give me Death!'

Well, they ended up in the Registry Office. He said he thought the Registrar was a Ventriloquist. They got married and lived unhappily ever after.

Harry Duff

Harry was a good friend of mine, we worked as welders in the boatyaird at the same time. Him and me used to go out drinking on Friday nights, then off to the Dancing at *The Pally* in Tay Street to see if we could get a lass. Usually by the time we got there, put our coats in the cloaky, and went down to the dance floor, it was time to go hame. Sometimes if we were lucky, we got a lass and took her hame. Well, the thing about Harry was that every time he got a lass (and that wasn't very often, and the same went for myself by the way) he always fell in love with them, and would make a date to take them to the pictures. When Harry went to meet them in the town at some bus stop or wherever, he was always getting stood up, or as we called it, 'getting duffed.' He never gave up, he always had faith in them turning up and he would stand there for long spells, waiting. One night he was standing at a bus stop in town, waiting for a lassie from Fintry to turn up. He had already been there for about an hour when I came along so, feeling sorry for him I said, 'Come on Harry, forget about her and let's go for a couple of pints.' He looked me straight in the eye, and he said, 'No, I'll give her another nineteen buses.'

Jim Gall

When I was a young lad my mates and I used to drink in a pub called Andy Laing's (its right name was The Five Dials and it's now called The Stobbie Bar). Well like all pubs it had its own characters and one of them was Jimmy Gall. He worked as a labourer with the platers in the boatyaird, and was in Andy Laing's most nights. He was a big man who sometimes wore a bowler hat and reminded me of Victor McLaglen, the film star who always played a big Irishman in early Hollywood movies.

Jim's regular habit on the cold winter nights was when there was a big coal fire burning in the pub. He would stand right in front of it toasting himself and have a good claw at his dowp, prior to letting loose a rip-roaring fart. You should have seen the expressions on his face, you would think he was in heaven.

Rumour has it that a couple of old lads lost their eyebrows while sitting too close to the fire as Jim Gall let a big sneaky one slide out.

Joe the Pole Taggerty

The influx of Poles coming into this country lately reminds me of a story Joe Taggerty told me years ago, in the boatyaird. Joe was a plater's helper there. Joe said that during the war Dundee was stacked with Poles, they were the ones who escaped from the Germans and landed here, and that one of their camps was on the Kingsway opposite Mid Craigie. Lots of Poles married local girls and settled here. They had their own club here. There was one who lived down the stairs from me and we just called him Felix. His Polish name was some length - it ran across the letter box, down the stairs and out the close, then onto the street.

The story Joe told was that, during the war the dance halls were full of Poles, and all the lassies were going for them. Their manners were exquisite, they had nice uniforms, and when they asked a lassie for a dance they would bow, click their heels and kiss the back of the lassie's hand. Well Joe knew some of the Polish soldiers and borrowed one their uniforms. So off he went to the dancing in his Polish uniform and his phoney accent. He said it worked for a couple of nights, getting himself a couple of lassies to take home but eventually he was found out.

Killer the Crane Driver

Killer was employed by the Dundee Harbour Board as a crane driver. He operated his crane to unload cargo from all types of ships, assisting the Dundee dockers, but they all felt uncomfortable working under him as he was a bit reckless. His crane jib used to slew all over the place, lifting and dropping containers, crashing and bumping cargo on the decks and nearly decapitating dockers. When Killer got early retirement from the Harbour Board you could hear a big sigh of relief from the docks.

Killer got himself a hobby – gardening. He had an allotment on Old Craigie Road and started off full of enthusiasm and big plans. Each day before commencing, he would have a couple of cans of beer, then another couple and then on and on. The place was littered with empty tins. People passing his plot thought he was growing tins, and that he was growing into a robot as he sat in his barrow, remembering the days when he worked in the harbour. I think he was evicted from his allotment in the end. And the last lift he saw was two skip-loads of empty tins being taken away from his plot.

Lavvies on the Stairs

Here's some more toilet humour. This story is about lavvies on the stair. If there was something people hated about the old days, it was sharing a lavvy with a few neighbours. They were dark dingy places, and when you had to go, as sure as fate, there was always someone else on the throne. So you would go back up to the house and stand behind the door and wait to hear the plug getting pulled. Once again you'd dash down the stairs, but about another half a dozen people had the same idea, so there would be a big melee on the stairs. Some people were in the toilet that long you thought they had taken root there, they must have had peens and needles when they stood up.

The boatyaird boys were lavvy dwellers as well. There was an old boatyaird joke about a boatyaird lad who died and went to heaven. When St Peter met him at the Pearly Gates, he asked where he worked, and the lad said that he had worked in the boatyaird. Peter says, 'Come in, there's loads o' boatyaird workers up here - awa you go and have walk, you'll find plenty of them.' The lad walked around for a couple hours then went back to St Peter and said, 'I canna find any boatyaird lads.' Peter said, 'Have you tried the lavvies?'.

Meh Granny's Floor

One of the funniest laughs I had as a young lad was at my Granny's house. My Granny lived in Catherine Street, in Stobswell. The family were having a farewell party for my Gran, as she was leaving for Australia to live with her son in Melbourne.

The party was going full swing in the ground-floor two-room flat. It was packed to the gunwales. My sister, brother and myself, and a load of our cousins were all there. Nearly all the parents and friends were a' snottering and greeting, singing sangs like 'Yer no awa tae bide awa', and 'Will ye no come back again.'

Meanwhile a' the bairns were jumping a' ower the place. Somebody then shouted, 'Thae bairns are driving me nuts! Send them a' ben the hoos!' Well, we were all dispatched ben the hoos where we all started jumping up and doon on wir Gran's big bed which was covered by all the guest's hats and coats or whatever. There was a big dresser at the bottom of the bed and one of my cousins suggested we climb on to the dresser and jump from it on to the bed, so we all lined up and took turns and I was last to jump. The next thing I knew was that there was an almighty crash and the whole floor collapsed, taking all us kids with it. We all thought we were going down under before our Gran. We couldn't see each other for dust and stoor and everybody's claes were covered wi' muck. Some of the mithers ran to see what happened to their little angels and nearly fell in the foundations too. We were dragged out one at a time, and we all got a doing (battering) while we ran the parental gauntlet. It was definitely the best perty eh was ever at.

Moothie Jean

Moothie Jean worked in Broaghies Mill on the Arbroath Road opposite Baffin Street. An old woman who worked there told me Moothie Jean was a cleaner in the mull lavvy. She was a wee skinny woman, wi' short hair and she always wore baffies or rovies, which were home-made hoos-shoes that were crocheted out of jute.

Well, when the women in the lavvy gathered to about half a dozen in numbers, oot would come Jean's moothie, and she would blast out a few tunes. They say she was a right rotten moothie player too. Some women said it was a ploy by the management to put her in the lavvy, thinking maybe if the women's spirits were flagging Moothie Jean would be giving them a booster to work harder. Or maybe the women would just be glad to get back to their looms to escape from Jean's unmelodic moothie playing.

Nobby

Nobby's a character you will see going about Dundee. I don't really know much about him, but to me he sticks out like sair thumb. He wears a big red Stetson cowboy hat most of the time, occasionally swapping it for a baseball cap or some kind of hat from Asia, but what you really notice about him is his jacket - it's covered with badges and medals of all sorts. His jacket may not be worth much but he would get a few pounds for it as scrap value, I suppose. He always reminds me of Bugs Bunny's arch enemy, Yosemite Sam.

I once did a drawing of Nobby which I've re-drawn and included here. Nobby must've duplicated the original drawing and put it about. If you were to go into some Dundee pubs, you might see the drawing of Nobby on the wall. I went into the Balmore Bar and noticed that there were about thirty drawings of Nobby all around the bar. He must've been going around Dundee with the drawings like he was selling the *Big Issue*.

Rossie the Barber

Rossie the Barber was in Dura Street, Stobswell and he epitomized everything a local barber shop should be. He would talk about any topic but his favourite subject was football and his team was Stobswell Juniors.

There was a lad getting his haircut from Rossie one day, and he said to Rossie, 'I haven't see you up watching Stobbie Football Club lately.' And Rossie, without a smile on his face replied, 'Well they never came up to see me when I was bad.'

As school lads, we had to go for a haircut after school because the mills came oot later-on and that was a busy time for Rossie. He had all the different magazines and papers in his shop. Some of them were ancient. He had this hair cream of his own make, and after a haircut he used to slap this cream on your head. When it dried later, it was like concrete. The top of your head felt like a toffee-aipple. In the summertime you would get seven weeks holiday from school, so you would get a haircut called a seeven-weeker, which would do you until you went back to school.

Safari Sam

Sam was a doorman at the Gaumont Cinema, which is now the Deja Vu Nightclub in the Coogate. This is a story I was told by an old lad a long time ago…

It seems the manager had this brilliant idea that involved Sam. The film which was on show that week was a jungle film all about Africa. So he asked Sam to get dressed up as a big-game hunter, and stand outside the cinema, as it would be good publicity. Sam told the manager to piss off, as it was February and the weather was atrocious. Sam said he couldn't stand outside in those conditions, it would freeze the baas aff him and was the manager aware that the local pawnbrokers were beginning to take in their signs?

Well the manager got his way by giving Sam another tenner on his wages and Sam was kitted-out and sent out into those perilous winter conditions. Alas, two days later Sam had succumbed to the elements and died from pneumonia. They say he must have had a big smile on his face as he lay in his coffin in the crematorium, as he was about to get a real big heat.

Tannadice

Tannadice is the home of Dundee United. Years ago when we were laddies we used to go there when they were in the Second Division, especially when the Reserves were playing. We used it as a playground. It was always empty at these games so we would run about mad on the terraces. It didn't seem to bother the players on the field, they were more interested in their game. We liked playing in the grand stand. It was just a big wooden shed. The United supporters, called it the hen-coop. When the ball would hit the stand, the stoor, dust, and pigeon shite came down and covered everybody. I liked United's colours in those days, it was black and white stripes.

I was told this story by an old supporter years ago... He was at a cup match one Saturday and United were playing St Johnstone. He said, every time the St Johnstone right-winger got the ball, he just raced past United's full-back. This happened time and time again. Well, this old United supporter who was standing at the wall next to the touchline got so fed up with it that the next time the St Johnstone player flew past United's full-back, the old guy was waiting, and when the St Johnstone winger was dead level with him, he whipped aff his bonnet and whacked the St Johnstone player over the head with it. They say the referee booked the old guy and the police cautioned him.

Tattie Howking

Once a year, school children were asked if they would like to go picking potatoes for a couple of weeks. Well most of them went including myself and it was torture, to me anyway. I went with The Stobbie Skail (Stobswell Secondary). We left the skail in buses like a load of refugees, and were drapped aff in some god-forsaken field miles from civilization.

They marked aff your bits (your section) where you were to pick, then the tractors took off. I think the drivers were all ex-racing drivers, and they just went roond and roond and roond, you could hardly stand up at piece-break. They had two tattie digger contraptions, one was called the 'Oliver.' It was like a conveyor belt, it left the tatties in a straight line but they were covered in earth so you still had to dig them out. The other machine was called the 'Scatterer,' and when it went past you got bombarded wi' tatties. One time, I had on a big pair of wellies and when the Scatterer went passed, my wellies got full to the brim with earth, tatties and stanes. Tattie picking was definitely no' for me.

The Battles of the Albert Bar

The Albert Bar had three regular characters who drank there. There was Tam, John, and wee Jimmy. The three always sat and drank together, telling jokes and having a good old laugh. Then later on when the drink got the better of them, the fighting would erupt. They would knock the stuffing out of each other. They reminded me of the Three Stooges that used to be on the films. Wee Jimmy always seemed to have a bag of messages with him, and they used to get scattered all over the pub. I don't think he used to get them all back. And later when the dust had settled, they just sat down and got back to their drinking as if it had never happened.

It happened that often, people in the pub never seemed to notice it.

The Bird Man

One day, I was working on the deck of a ship in the boatyaird when I noticed a painter. He was painting the hand-rails on the ship and every time a seagull flew past, he would put his paintbrush down, stand erect and salute the seagull. Well what happened next was, somebody threw a load of bread into the water and a big flock of seagulls started flying about. The Bird Man was saluting like hell and his arm was going up and down like the clappers. The last thing I saw of him was the gaffer and another lad leading him away from his paintbrush. I never saw him in the boatyaird again.

The Dundee Courier - Tap O The Hull

A good few years ago, two women worked in the launderette at the tap o' the hull. They were a right couple o' gas-bags, and you couldna go past that shop withoot getting a good blethering to. One of them we used to call the Dundee Courier because of her local newsworthiness. The Hulltoon was a busy place and they spent a lot of time just watching passers-by, and they wanted to know the ins-and-outs of anything and everything. They would point to people passing by and say stuff like, 'Who's that?' and, 'Who's she going with now?' and, 'She's expecting again!' You almost had to get down on your hands and knees and crawl past their window to escape detection, but if you happened to pass the shop and got captured or waylaid, you would get a severe grilling.

The Italian Match

I was told this tall tale from Charlie from Lochee. People from that area will know who I am writing about. Anyway he told me this story about two Italian football teams that were made up from the community of chip shop owners, ice cream shops and cafes.

The two teams arranged to play their match on the Cowp (riverside pitches) which was often surfaced with danders or cinders instead of grass. Well, when the two teams arrived, they found that the pitch hadn't been marked-out with the usual lines of sawdust, so they marked the pitches out themselves - with fritters. When the match was eventually finished, a flock of seagulls swooped down and cleaned up all the lines of fritters.

CABRELLI
DORA
FORTE
SOAVE
SCHIAVETTA
SCIORTINO
FRANCHI ZACCARINI ZANRE FUGACCIA ESPOSITO
BASTIANELLO CAPATELLI VISOCCHI MORTALI BENEDETTI
VETTRAINO IANNETTA BASTIANELLI
PALADINI PACIONE
RONCONE
HALF TIME
CONES AND SLIDER
VISOCCHI'S

The Mary Rose

During the Kestrel Days there was a lot of friction between the different departments in the works. Platers didn't get on with the welders and the plumbers were always at loggerheads with platers.

Stevie, the plater's shop-steward was always arguing with Geordie, the plumbers shop-steward. Stevie would always say to Geordie, 'You never seem to do any work,' and Geordie would always say the same to Stevie.

Anyway they were both in the canteen one day, Stevie was reading the paper. The headlines declared that the *Mary Rose*, the warship of Henry the VIII of England had just been raised. It had sunk off Southsea on the 19th of July 1545. Stevie then said, 'They also found Geordie's tool box on board and it had never ever been opened.'

The Seagull

This is a story told to me by (The Laird of Lochee) Charlie Walker. Charlie said when he was younger he played in goal for some local football team. He said he was called the Cat, and the only way you could get him off the goal-line, was to put a saucer of milk on the penalty spot.

He said there were two teams playing on the Cowp football pitches. One of the players ran down the wing and crossed the ball over the goalmouth but at that moment a seagull was diving down to grab a bit of bread near the goal. A striker ran into the box as the ball was coming over and, leaping into the air with a beautiful header, he nutted the seagull into the back of the net.

The Three Whoppers

There were three lads in the boatyaird who would tell great-big whoppers. One was Wullie (I can't recall his surname), the other two were Joey Hart and Jeemie Mann.

Well Wullie said to Joey and Jeemie, 'I was drinking in Perth on Saturday and I missed the last bus and had to walk home. But my brither (Brother) was with me and he was drunk, so I got him on my shithers (shoulders) and walked right to Beechwood.' Joey said, 'The same thing happened to me about a month ago. Missed the last bus from Perth, the brither was drunk, on the shithers wi' him, and walked right to Fintry.' Up pops Jeemie and says, 'Funny, the same thing happened to me about a fortnight ago. Missed the last bus from Perth, brither drunk, on the shithers wi' him, and walked right back to Douglas wi' him slavering doon meh back.' Wullie jumps in and says, 'Wait a meenit you twa, yi didna let me finish meh story! When eh walked hame from Perth wi' meh brither, eh didna tell ye he had his accordion wi' him, did I?'

The Berries

I remember when I was young, we used to take off to the berries in the summertime. If we were lucky we got to Blairgowrie - the klondyke of the berryfields. They used to say the berries were just hinging aff the bushes there. Well I couldn't imagine them hinging any place else.

Wir mithers made oor pieces up. We always seemed to have the same meat-paste ingredients on our pieces, and a bottle o' Barries lemonade which I thought was the best lemonade in the land.

You could pick berries that you put in small baskets that were then sent off to make jam but you were better off on buckets, because these berries were sent off to make dye. You could put a stane in the berry-bucket to make it seem heavier, but you had to watch at the weighing of the berries that they didn't spot the stane or you would be in big trouble. Our best trick was just to pee in the buckets of berries.

The Dundee Eskimo

A long time ago Dundee was a great whaling port and the harbour was filled with whaling ships. It must have been a great sight, and the men who sailed them must have been (as they say) tough as teak. The story I tell you now was actually true (I think).

A skipper of a whaling ship met and became friends with an Eskimo and he invited him back to Dundee for a wee holiday. When he arrived in Dundee he was treated as a celebrity and shown all the local hot-spots (That would be the pubs in the Overgate I suppose). They put him up in a garret in the Overgate, where he caught the cauld. He couldn't get rid of it and his nose was snottering for weeks. So he bade farewell to Dundee and went back to the Arctic but, unlike the song, 'Am No Awa Tae Bide Awa' he sang the opposite – 'Eh'm Awa Tae Bide Awa.'

The Lord Provost's Chairs

I was told this story a long time ago by an ex-skaffy but whether it's true or not I don't know.

A skaffy larry was doing the rounds in the town centre picking up rubbish from outside the shops, then made its way into the city square to pick up more stuff. The skaffies spotted a pile of chairs sitting outside the City Chambers so they wheeched them on to the skaffy-larry and away with them.

What they didn't know was, the City Chambers had been getting a clean-out and the chairs had been put outside to get a wee airing.

As luck would have it, the chairs were rescued by a keen civic type, just before they were dumped on the Cowp.

The Peek

There was a picture house in Dundee called 'The Palladium' which was nicknamed, 'The Peek.' It was situated in Alexander Street, and it was something to behold. It was built half by brick and half riggily tin (corrugated iron). You could smell its mankyness before you could see it. It was said that The Peek was so dirty, that the mice in there wore boiler-suits. It cost a three-penny bit (three old pence) to get in, and the seating was just wooden forms. The feature films changed three times a week, and they had the chapters (serials). When a film was on, it was absolute bedlam, you couldn't hear a thing! Everybody was shouting fighting and peeing. Yes, lots of the kids just peed where they were. If you wanted a wee tub of ice cream and you couldn't afford a whole one, they would cut it and sell you half a tub.

A friend of mine said he was in The Peek one night sitting on the end of the form when something flashed by him heading down the aisle, followed by a loud crash. What happened was that some old lad was sleeping in his wheelchair when somebody let his brakes off. Seemingly this happened regularly to this old lad.

They say some gent came up from London to take over the management of The Palladium in Dundee with out ever setting eyes on it. He arrived in Dundee and hailed a taxi to take him to The Palladium. They say he never even got out of the taxi, and it's said he was on the next train back to London.

Tinky

A lot of Dundee men were working down in Redcar where an oil rig was being built. One of the Dundee lads who went to Redcar was called Tinky. He was earning good money, there were plenty of local pubs and clubs to spend their wages in, and Tinky was out socialising every night. Lodgings were hard to get there, and in those days they crammed everybody they could into the digs. Sometimes you were lucky and you would get a single bed. If not, some lads had to share a double bed with their work-mate.

Tinky met this Weegie (Glaswegian) lad on the job and they became bosom pals and found they shared hobbies such as boozing and bed wetting (doing 'dampers' as we used to call it). Well they ended up sharing the same bed. Well the story goes that every time they got pished, they got pishing, and they also had a wee spew now and again (some lads referred to their bed as the Big Muddy). They were in that bed 'til they were laid off, and that wasn't long in coming. I think the landlady dumped their bed in the backyard and when it was dried out, she cremated it.

Tippy Tumbles

Tippy Tumbles was a woman who drank in The Albert Bar. She was a nice woman, but when she had a good drink on her, she could be a right nippy-sweetie. She was very small, and she had this massive head of curls. She must have been in her sixties when she drank in The Albert, yet she always had on this mini skirt, and great big white high heelers. Anyway, when she had a good fizzer she would get the barman to phone her a taxi. When the taxi arrived, she would head for the door. Then you would see her party piece. She would trip and tumble towards the door then 'bang' she would end up headering the door and knocking herself out. They say it happened more than once or twice. By the way, her nippy pal was called Keyhole Kate.

Wee Jeemie The Mountain Goat

Wee Jeemie worked in the boatyaird as a labourer. He used to pass me on the street going to his work in the morning. He would run for about twenty yards at a trot, then walk for twenty yards. He used to repeat this process until he got to the boatyaird. He was a poor looking soul, always needing a haircut with hairs sprouting out of every orifice. Well, Jeemie got himself involved with the First Aid Dept. The First Aid squad trained in the yaird some nights after the workers went home. They were assembled on the jetty beside a ship berthed there. They needed a volunteer to go down to the engine room and then they would go down with the stretcher and rescue him. So they picked Jeemie. 'Right Jeemie, go down to the engine room, lie down some place and just pretend you have been knocked out. 'We'll come down and rescue you.' So after 10 minutes they went onboard, and down to the engine room to rescue Jeemie. An hour and a half later they were still searching for him, shouting and calling his name and lots of other names as well. Eventually, one of the lads found him lying on top of some pipes. Somebody shouted, 'You little shite, we've been looking for you for ages! Did you no' hear us shouting? Why didn't you answer us?' Jeemie said, 'You said I was knocked out, and if I was, I couldna hear ye could I?' Somebody else shouted, 'Knock the little shite out for real!'

I think they punted him from the First Aid team after that.

Wee Jimmy and Sharing the Load

I was raised in the Stobswell area of Dundee, close to The Puir Hoos (The Poor House), later known as The Rowans. There were some unfortunate people who lived there. The men all wore the same suits made of the roughest materials, and the women had some dresses made of the same materials. The place was like some old Charles Dickens story. My pal's father was the head gardener there and sometimes we were allowed in. I remember one day, my pal and I walked through the dining hall as they were all having dinner - men on one side, women on the other (with large portraits of the benefactor and the governor looking down on them), and these poor unfortunate souls were all eating in an eerie silence. It's an experience I have never forgotten.

Now let's have a wee story about one of the characters from there. Wee Jimmy was sometimes sent down to Wallace's 'Land O' Cakes' for some extra pehs and bridies on Saturday mornings. Well the women in shop would load up a pie-board and help lift it onto Wee Jimmy's head so that he could carry it easily. Wee Jimmy would then head up Eliza Street towards The Puir Hoos, on Mollison Street. Well halfway up the road Jimmy must have thought he was getting stronger, as his load was getting lighter because the local kids were pinching his pehs and bridies from the board as he passed them by. When he arrived at The Puir Hoos he wouldn't have had many pehs and bridies left (the puir bugger). Eventually he was relieved of that duty.

Wee Joey

Wee Joey lived in Mid Craigie with his mother and sister. He was the apple of his mother's eye and he was spoiled rotten by her. You would have thought he was ten feet tall the way he went about, and he thought he knew it all. Well Joey's big night was when he came home from the boatyaird with his pay on a Friday. He would have a bath which had been prepared for him by his sister. Her big chore for him on a Friday was to have all his clobber ready. Everything was laid out on the bed - his suit lay on the bed, tie and shirt, and his shoes polished and on the floor. His niece once told me it was like a little man lying on the bed. Washed and dressed, 'Wee' Joey was ready for his 'Big' time on the town.

Wull the Grieve

Wull the Grieve was an engineer who worked in the boatyaird boilershop - a part of the boatyaird where the boilers for ships were made. They fitted out the engines there, the ships' funnels were made there, and it was a busy place in its heyday. There were a large number of men working in the boilershop, so the toilets were a very busy place. Every time Wull went to the toilets, they were full.

Wull was a bit o' a teuchter. He lived in the country some place and he kept ferrets. One day, he took his ferrets to work with him. When he went to the toilet later on in the day it was the same as usual - a full house. So he let his ferrets loose in the toilet. A couple of seconds later, he had the place to himself.

Wullie the Plumber

Wullie was a jazz drummer and a plumber in the boatyaird. In his spare time he liked a wee bit of the tea leafing (stealing) out of the big stores. One Saturday Wullie was in one of the big stores and he was looking for a shifter (adjustable spanner). Well when he got one, he stuck it up his jumper and was then spotted by a security man. So Wullie took to his heels up and doon the aisles. He evaded the security man eventually, but before doing so, he managed to slip the spanner beside the baked beans display.

Later on, they said an auld wummin was checking out with her baked beans and her shifting spanner and she told the check out girl that she thought it was a free offer of a newfangled tin opener that came with the beans.